W9-AXB-406

DISCARD

DK eyewonder

Ancient
Rome

LONDON, NEW YORK, MUNICH,
MELBOURNE, and DELHI

Written and edited by Lorrie Mack
Designed by Clare Shedden
Additional design Andrew Nash
Publishing manager Bridget Giles
Art director Rachael Foster
Jacket design Natalie Godwin
Jacket editor Mariza O'Keefe
Picture researcher Liz Moore
Production editor Sean Daly
Production controller Pip Tinsley
Consultant Angus Konstam

REVISED EDITION
DK UK
Senior editor Caroline Stamps
Senior art editor Rachael Grady
US editor Margaret Parrish
Jacket editor Manisha Majithia
Jacket designer Natasha Rees
Jacket design development manager
Sophia M. Tampakopoulos Turner
Producer (print production) Mary Slater
Producer (pre-production) Francesca Wardell
Publisher Andrew Macintyre

DK INDIA
Senior editor Shatarupa Chaudhuri
Senior art editor Rajnish Kashyap
Assistant editor Suneha Dutta
Art editor Isha Nagar
Managing editor Alka Thakur Hazarika
Managing art editor Romi Chakraborty
DTP designer Dheeraj Singh
Picture researcher Sumedha Chopra

First American Edition, 2009
This American Edition, 2014
Published in the United States by DK Publishing
4th floor, 345 Hudson Street
New York, New York 10014
14 15 16 17 10 9 8 7 6 5 4 3 2
002—196176—02/2014

Contents

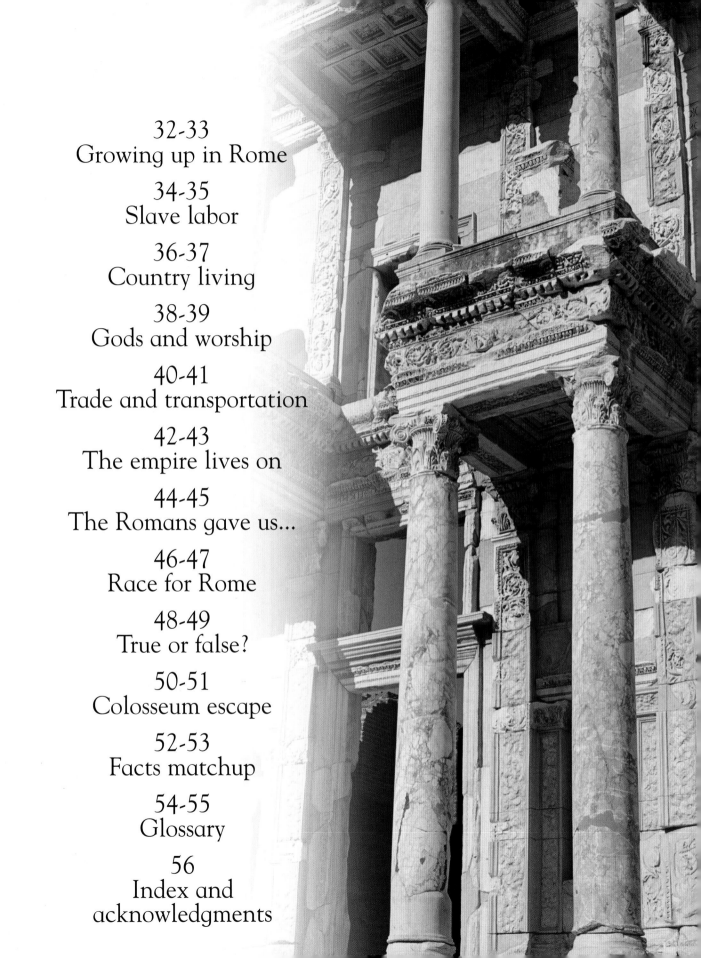

Welcome to ancient Rome

According to myth, Rome was founded by Romulus and Remus, twin sons of war god Mars. They built a great city, but in the end, they quarreled, and Romulus killed Remus. Rome is named after Romulus.

Two brothers
When they were born, Romulus and Remus were left on the banks of the Tiber River to die. They were found by a she-wolf, who fed them until a shepherd came to their rescue and raised them as his own.

The last king
Early Rome was ruled by kings. In 509 BCE, the last king, named Tarquin the Proud (above), was banished. Rome then became a republic—a place where power is held by the people, or by the representatives they elect.

Eternal city
Built on seven hills near the Tiber River, Rome was the biggest city in the ancient world, and it is still a thriving capital city thousands of years later.

Life at the top

During the Republic, Rome was governed by a group of noblemen called the Senate, led by two consuls. They shared the job of governing and were elected every year. Later, Rome was ruled by emperors (see pages 18-19).

Some citizens had bronze copies made of their citizenship documents.

Who's who?

People in ancient Rome were either citizens, who were free and could vote, or slaves, who were owned by other people (see pages 34-35). To be a citizen you had to appear on the official census.

Census taking shown on a stone relief from the Temple of Neptune in Rome

Good neighbors

Rome was heavily influenced by two of its neighbors—the Greeks and the Etruscans. Both were older cultures that produced great artists, architects, and scholars. Greek and Etruscan religions also affected Roman beliefs.

Etruscan musicians shown on a 5th-century BCE tomb fresco

Grand Roman buildings reflect the style of Greece. This is the Parthenon, near Athens.

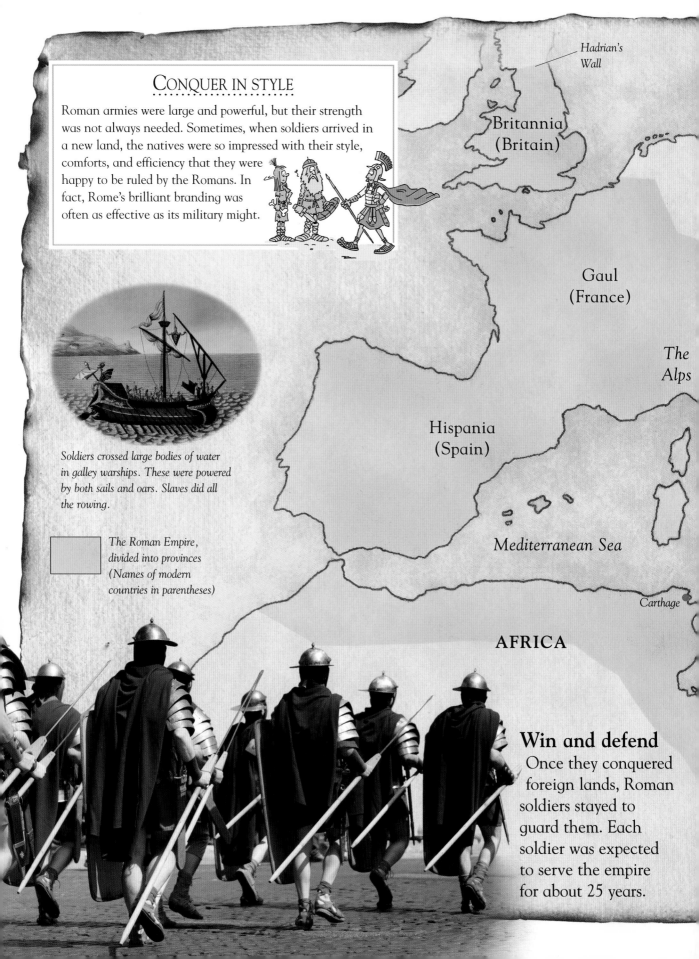

CONQUER IN STYLE

Roman armies were large and powerful, but their strength was not always needed. Sometimes, when soldiers arrived in a new land, the natives were so impressed with their style, comforts, and efficiency that they were happy to be ruled by the Romans. In fact, Rome's brilliant branding was often as effective as its military might.

Soldiers crossed large bodies of water in galley warships. These were powered by both sails and oars. Slaves did all the rowing.

The Roman Empire, divided into provinces (Names of modern countries in parentheses)

Hadrian's Wall

Britannia
(Britain)

Gaul
(France)

The
Alps

Hispania
(Spain)

Mediterranean Sea

Carthage

AFRICA

Win and defend

Once they conquered foreign lands, Roman soldiers stayed to guard them. Each soldier was expected to serve the empire for about 25 years.

The Roman Empire

Five hundred years after the founding of Rome, Roman armies had taken over most of the world that was known at the time, from Egypt to present-day Britain. Rome had more wealth and power than any nation, anywhere, ever.

Germania
(Germany)

Dating from around 63 BCE, this copper coin displays the head of Emperor Augustus.

Constantinople was named after Emperor Constantine I, who brought Christianity to Rome.

●ROME

(Italy)

Graecia
(Greece)

Constantinople
(Istanbul)

The Roman Empire reached its height in the 2nd century CE.

When the Romans conquered Greece, they adopted Greek art and culture. This Roman arch was built in the Greek style in Leptis Magna, present-day Libya, north Africa.

Aegyptus
(Egypt)

The empire strikes out!

In their struggle to expand and defend their empire, the Romans fought huge, bloody battles and short skirmishes (small battles). Sometimes they lost, but much more often, they were victorious.

At one time, there were about 375,000 men in the Roman army.

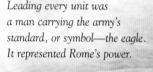

Leading every unit was a man carrying the army's standard, or symbol—the eagle. It represented Rome's power.

Carved in stone
The Picts carved these strange stone slabs over many centuries. They are the only visual record we have of Pictish culture.

Computer reconstruction of Hadrian's Wall

Take your Pict
The Romans invaded Britain, but they could not control the Caledonians (Picts), an ancient tribe in the north—what is now Scotland. In the second century CE, the Roman Emperor Hadrian built an enormous wall to keep them out and to mark the empire's boundary. Parts of it are still standing.

The fight for Gaul

From 58 to 52 BCE, the Romans fought to control Gaul (modern-day France). They succeeded spectacularly because Julius Caesar had many friends in Gaul. Also, many Gallic soldiers served in his legions, and several Gallic tribes asked for his help in their battles with other Gallic tribes.

The Gallic leader Vercingetorix surrendering to Caesar

At the end, there were enough bodies left on the battlefield to make the soil extremely fertile for years.

Battle of Arausio

Rome was not always triumphant. This earlier action in Gaul in 105 BCE resulted in the total defeat of Rome by the Cimbri, a northern tribe. As a result, Roman legions were reorganized to make them even more deadly.

Battle of Actium

In the sea near Greece, the forces of Augustus Caesar fought those of Antony and Cleopatra in 31 BCE. Some of Antony's men deserted because they hated Cleopatra, and some of Cleopatra's men ran home to Egypt. Caesar won.

Fighting back

With its incredible power and wealth, Rome had plenty of enemies. Some brave souls defended their people against the powerful invader, while others attacked the mighty empire itself.

Royal warrior

Boudicca was queen of the Iceni, a Celtic tribe in Roman Britain. After her husband's death, the Romans stole her lands and robbed her people. In 60 to 61 CE, her army destroyed a Roman legion and burned several Roman cities. When she was finally defeated, she killed herself by taking poison.

Nile queen

By joining forces with Julius Caesar, and later Mark Antony, Egyptian Queen Cleopatra hoped to gain power over Rome. But Caesar was murdered, and Antony killed himself. So, in 30 BCE, Cleopatra ended her own life by letting a poisonous snake bite her.

Cleopatra

Enter the barbarians

The Goths were German barbarians (uncivilized people)—one tribe was called the Visigoths (west Goths). In 408 CE, the Visigoth king, Alaric, marched his army to Rome and eventually conquered it. This was the beginning of the end of the Roman Empire.

Hannibal took 15 days to cross the Alps.

After defeating Rome, Hannibal was made emperor of Carthage, and his face was put on the coins of Carthage.

Marching to victory

Hannibal was a general from neighboring Carthage. In 218 BCE, he marched toward Rome from the north by crossing the Alps with 100,000 men and 40 elephants. Although he lost thousands of men and most of the elephants, he still inflicted crushing defeats on the Roman army.

Some fought Rome with armies, others with complex plots.

Hannibal facts

● Historians have said that ancient Rome feared only two enemies: Cleopatra and Hannibal.

● Hannibal was famous for saying, "We will either find a way, or make one."

● Hannibal was celebrated for his brilliant battle plans, and he is sometimes called "the father of strategy."

The soldier's art

Rome's power came from its armies. These were called legions, and Roman soldiers were known as legionaries. Possibly the most successful armies of all time, they were made up of citizens who joined voluntarily and were issued with fine uniforms and weapons.

Legionary

A soldier's helmet protected his face, head, and neck.

Where's the boss?
Legionaries carried huge wooden shields for protection. The handle in the middle had a metal cover on the outside, called a boss. This could be used to strike any enemy who got too close.

Soldiers would hang cups and a leather bottle of water or wine from their packs.

Shoulder packs
Legionaries were given large sacks to carry all their equipment and supplies—when they were full, these weighed up to 90 lb (40 kg).

Spear

Weapons
Originally, legionaries carried thick spears designed for stabbing (far left). Later designs with a narrow point (left) were intended for throwing. These could pierce both shields and armor.

Standard bearer

Archer

Centurion

Just the job

Each legion had an emblem, or standard, carried by a standard bearer. Special soldiers called archers used bows and arrows. Each band of 100 men—a centuria—was led by a centurion.

Straps lapped each other to lace up.

Armor was made from metal strips fastened with leather, or leather and rope.

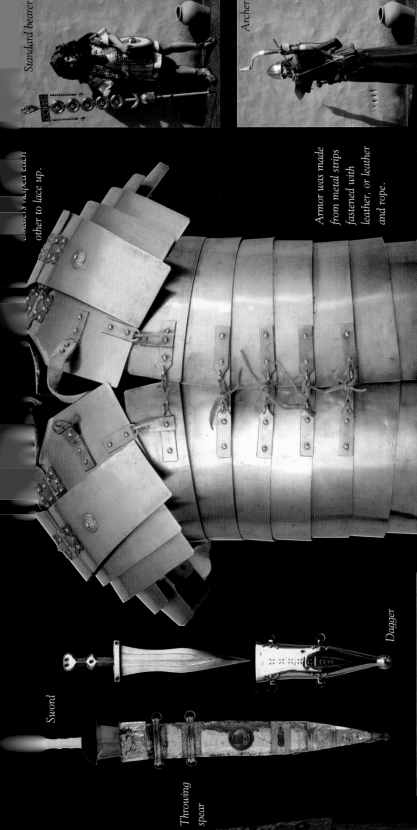

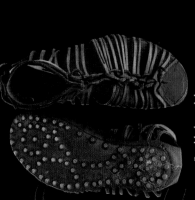

Studded sandals

Sword

Dagger

Throwing spear

Making camp

When legionaries were on the march, they stopped at night to make camp. In about six hours, they could build a complex city.

The army in action

While the Roman army was led by its legions, backup was supplied by auxiliary regiments. These soldiers were not Roman citizens, but subjects from conquered lands, promised citizenship for their service. Together, the legions and the auxiliaries were almost unbeatable.

Ballistas were made in different sizes.

Throwing stones

One important weapon for Roman legionaries was the ballista—a type of catapult. This worked like a large crossbow to shoot arrows or stone balls.

Roman catapults were based on a Greek design.

Left, right, left

Roman legionaries were highly organized and disciplined. They marched in step and moved as one unit in response to blasts from a trumpet.

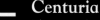 **Centuria**
There were between 80 and 100 legionaries in a centuria.

   **Manipulus**
160-200 legionaries

On their horses

Although they were auxiliary troops, the cavalry (soldiers on horseback) were paid extra because they had to supply their own horses. They went ahead of the legions as guards and scouts. This carving is from the tomb of a Roman officer.

Under siege

Auxiliary troops built siege towers— wheeled wooden structures that could be rolled up to enemy walls.

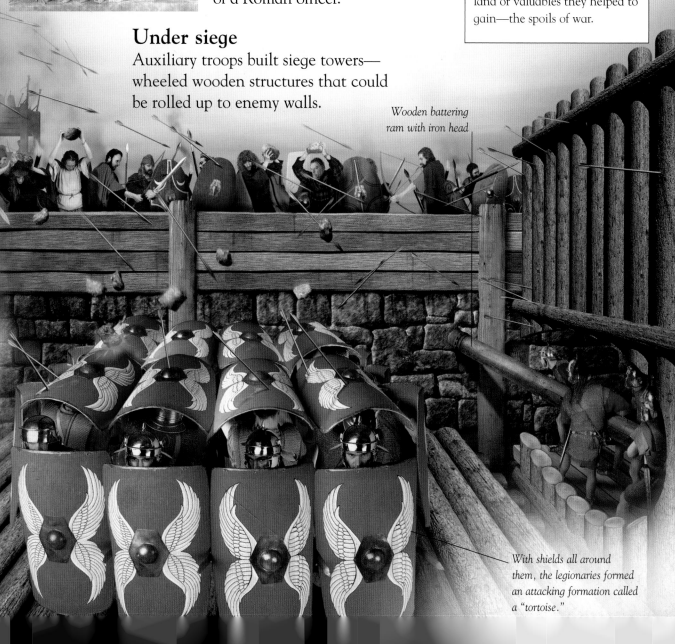

Wooden battering ram with iron head

With shields all around them, the legionaries formed an attacking formation called a "tortoise."

A day in the life...

In Roman towns and cities, street life was much like it is for us—people took walks, shopped, and stopped for a drink. Some everyday Roman activities, though, are less common today—such as reading the future in fish guts.

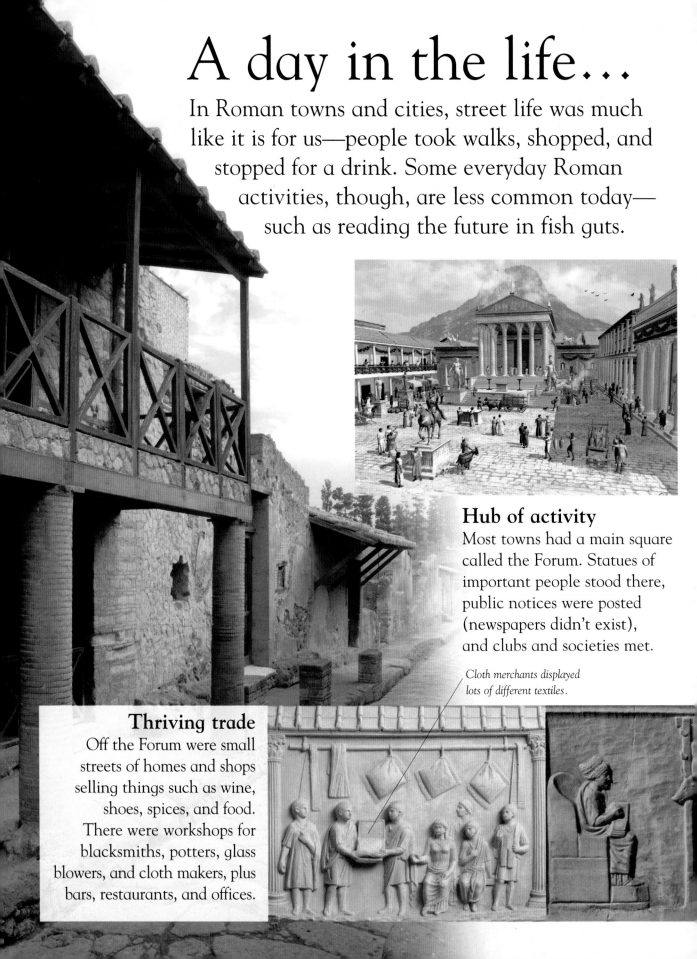

Hub of activity

Most towns had a main square called the Forum. Statues of important people stood there, public notices were posted (newspapers didn't exist), and clubs and societies met.

Cloth merchants displayed lots of different textiles.

Thriving trade

Off the Forum were small streets of homes and shops selling things such as wine, shoes, spices, and food. There were workshops for blacksmiths, potters, glass blowers, and cloth makers, plus bars, restaurants, and offices.

Roads in Rome

Urban roads (paved, bricked, or left as dusty ground) were often dirty or flooded, so the paths on each side were raised. Huge stepping-stones allowed people to cross from one side to the other.

Looking to the future

Romans visited fortune-tellers for guidance about business, romance, or travel. Fortune-tellers could "read" the future by watching birds, lightning, or other natural events. Sometimes they found answers by gutting a fish and examining its insides.

Black as night

Towns and cities were very scary after dark. Romans lit their rooms, but the rough, dirty streets were almost pitch-black, with no police to keep people safe.

PUBLIC GATHERINGS

One convenience we share with the ancient Romans is the public restroom. Their public restrooms, however, were considerably *more* public than ours. Instead of separate cubicles, Roman facilities consisted of rows of holes where people sat next to their neighbors. Instead of paper, they used a sponge on the end of a stick.

Roman butchers used tools that looked just like ours.

Food was displayed appealingly to tempt customers.

Meet the emperors

Julius Caesar was a brilliant soldier who conquered many lands and peoples for the empire. He declared himself absolute ruler in 44 BCE. Soon after, he was murdered by a group of senators, who declared Rome to be a republic once again.

"Little Boots"

Rome's third emperor, Gaius (37–41 CE), was nicknamed Caligula, which means "Little Boots." Caligula is best known as a lunatic—he thought he was a god and threatened to make his favorite horse a consul. He acquired his affectionate nickname when he was a little boy—traveling with his father, he liked to dress in a child-sized army uniform.

Cruel leader

Septimus Severus (above) was declared emperor in 195 BCE after a bloody civil war. A ruthless fighter and efficient leader (*severus* is Latin for cruel), he may have inspired the name of the character Severus Snape in the *Harry Potter* books.

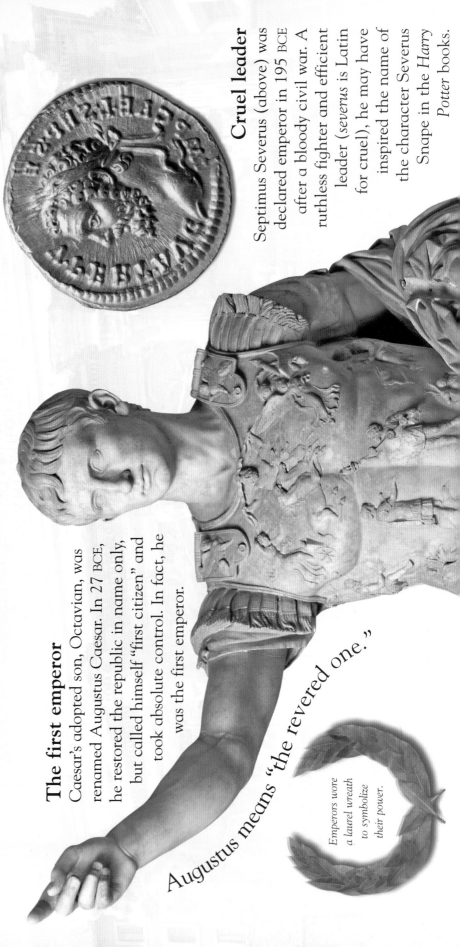

The first emperor

Caesar's adopted son, Octavian, was renamed Augustus Caesar. In 27 BCE, he restored the republic in name only, but called himself "first citizen" and took absolute control. In fact, he was the first emperor.

Augustus means "the revered one."

Emperors wore a laurel wreath to symbolize their power.

Only emperors were allowed to wear purple.

Dawn of Christianity

A great military leader, Constantine I (reigned 324-337 CE) turned Rome to Christianity. He took elements of the old Sun worship—such as the birthday of the Sun on December 25—into the new religion.

Literary leader

Marcus Aurelius (reigned 161-180 CE) was a weak, troubled emperor, but a very good and intelligent man. He wrote a book of philosophy, *The Meditations*, which is still respected today.

The year of four

Between 68 and 69 CE, four emperors ruled Rome. The first, Galba, was murdered by Otho. Otho killed himself when he was defeated by Vittellius. Vittellius was killed by his own army (above), which supported Vespasian. Vespasian ruled for 10 years.

At home in Rome

The wealthiest Romans had fabulous houses called villas, which were decorated with fine paintings and mosaics. Ordinary families lived in simpler houses, but many poor people lived in shabby apartment buildings.

Tile art
The Romans loved mosaics—intricate decorations made with pieces of tiles or glass. Mosaics can take the form of repeating designs or lifelike pictures.

A single mosaic tile is called a tessera—the plural is tesserae.

The entrance to a grand villa might have featured a mosaic dog to warn intruders that a ferocious beast was on guard!

Modern conveniences
Wealthy Romans were very comfortable at home—they had beautiful furnishings and lots of luxuries, such as running water and central heating.

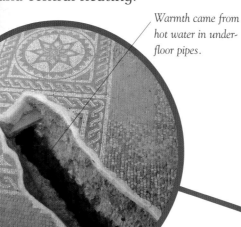

Warmth came from hot water in under-floor pipes.

Windows were just holes in the wall, with no shutters to keep out the cold and rain.

Crowded spaces

Many people lived in multistory apartment buildings (often above stores) called *insulae*. These were cramped, dark, overcrowded, and often dangerous.

Insulae were mostly made of wood. They often caught fire or collapsed.

Open to the sky

Typical villas were built around a central courtyard (the *atrium*), with a formal garden behind (the *peristylium*). Windows looked onto one of these—none faced the street.

Fast-food empire

Poor families had no space for cooking, so they bought ready-made meals from a Roman takeout. These ruins show how the food was displayed.

Some people think of Roman interiors as pale and restrained. In fact, they were richly colored and adorned with beautiful pictures painted directly onto wet plaster.

21

At their leisure

Ancient Romans had no television, DVDs, or computer games, but they loved going to the theater, gladiator fights, and chariot races. They also enjoyed playing sports and dice games.

Winner takes all

One popular pastime was competing at board games that involved throwing dice. (Their dice were just like ours.) Romans loved to gamble and would lay bets on most games and sports.

Roman dice were made from wood, ivory, bone, or stone.

Grace vs. strength

The Romans adopted the sport of wrestling from the Greeks. Both Greeks and Romans allowed only upper-body contact, but the Romans valued strength and force over the skill and grace prized by the Greeks.

Like gladiators, charioteers were often former slaves.

Chariot teams each had their own color—green, white, red, or blue.

Wheels on fire

At the racetrack, four teams of horses ran around an oval course. The tight turns at each end were the most dangerous part. Sometimes the chariot would fall and the horses or the rider would be killed.

The ancient world's a stage

Romans enjoyed many performing arts, from music and dancing to plays. They particularly enjoyed mime—an informal mix of words, music, and dance that appeared in the street or at home.

Roman street musicians are shown in this mosaic, which adorns a Pompeiian villa.

Actors often wore masks to show whether their character was tragic or comic.

At the theater

Admission to Roman theaters was free—everyone could watch formal plays, concerts, and pantomimes (which were a little like masked ballets with one main performer). The audience sat in tiered seats that allowed everyone to see, and they could hear every whisper on the stage.

In Roman theater, only men performed—women weren't allowed.

23

The Colosseum, the largest arena, could seat 50,000 people!

Roman arenas had lots of stairs, corridors, and entrances so people could enter and exit easily.

Animals on display

Wild animals such as lions, tigers, and bears fought both gladiators and other animals. Sometimes, they were placed in the ring simply to slaughter unarmed prisoners.

Thumbs UP!

A wounded gladiator could appeal to the emperor and crowd for mercy. If they put their thumbs up, the contest was stopped. If their thumbs went down, the gladiator was killed.

Killing for show

Romans, and their emperors, loved to watch people fight to the death in huge arenas. The men who put on this bloody show were prisoners or slaves trained in combat— the gladiators.

Sometimes the arena was flooded so gladiators could fight mock sea battles.

Wild animals were housed underneath the arena.

A gladiator who used a net to catch his opponent and a long fork to kill him was called a retiarius (net man).

Image is everything
Some gladiators took on specific roles—one who fought animals was called a *bestiarius* (animal man).

The floor of the arena would be covered in sand to soak up the blood.

Bath time

Roman bath houses were much more than places to wash. Here, at the end of the workday, people would relax with friends, enjoy beauty and health treatments, exercise, and play sports.

Grand baths were adorned with marble, mosaics, and murals.

All change

Visitors undressed and left their clothes in changing rooms. Possessions were often stolen, though, so slaves were made to guard them. If you didn't have your own slave, you could hire one at the baths.

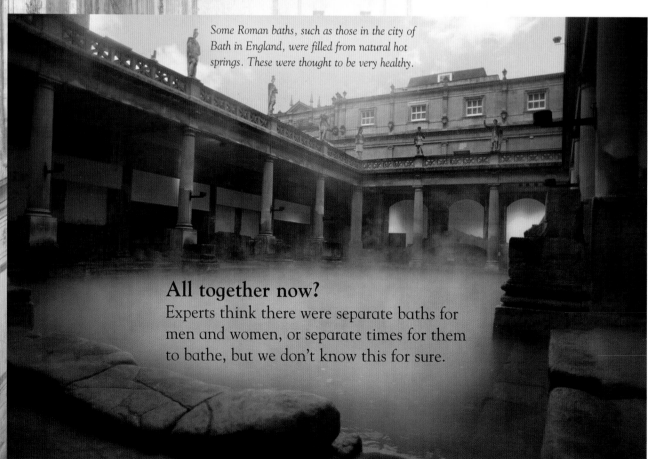

Some Roman baths, such as those in the city of Bath in England, were filled from natural hot springs. These were thought to be very healthy.

All together now?

Experts think there were separate baths for men and women, or separate times for them to bathe, but we don't know this for sure.

Dealing with dirt

There was no soap in ancient Rome. Bathers rubbed olive oil all over their bodies, then scraped it off with a curved, rounded blade called a *strigil*. Sometimes slaves would do this job for them.

Oil flask

Strigils were made from metal or bone.

Health and fitness

In addition to soaking in the bath, visitors could exercise, lift weights, and compete in athletic contests. Massages were popular, and these too might have been done by a personal slave or one provided by the bath house.

Roman workout gear would look very stylish on a modern beach!

Palm branches were given as prizes.

To keep in shape, Roman ladies lifted weights, threw the discus, and played ball games.

Keeping up appearances

Ancient Roman fashion didn't change quickly like fashion does today, but clothes and accessories served the same functions—they covered people up, kept them warm, and made them look nice.

Timeless style
With her softly curled hair and pretty gold jewelry, a wealthy Roman woman would not look out of place in the modern world.

This colored-wax portrait comes from the case of a mummy from Roman-period Egypt.

Found in a grave, this ivory comb was more likely to be used for finding lice than for grooming.

The carving reads "Modestina, farewell."

Women's wear
Women wore simple straight tunics called *stolas*—often a short one layered on top of a long one. These could be white, but they were often colored. Some ladies also wore a *palla*—a simple toga.

Baubles and bangles

Ordinary women wore jewelry made of amber, which was cheap and easily available. Wealthy women wore gold and precious stones.

This pure-gold snake armlet dates from the 1st century BCE.

Strung with garnet beads, this necklace is set in gold.

Many women had their ears pierced for earrings.

Grooming set

Found in Roman ruins in the UK, these tools include tweezers, a pumice stone for smoothing rough skin, and an earwax scoop.

STREET COLLECTIONS

To process their wool, cloth manufacturers (called fullers) needed a chemical called ammonia, which is found in urine. To take advantage of this natural resource, they would leave a bowl outside their workshop so passers-by could relieve themselves and provide a supply of ammonia at the same time.

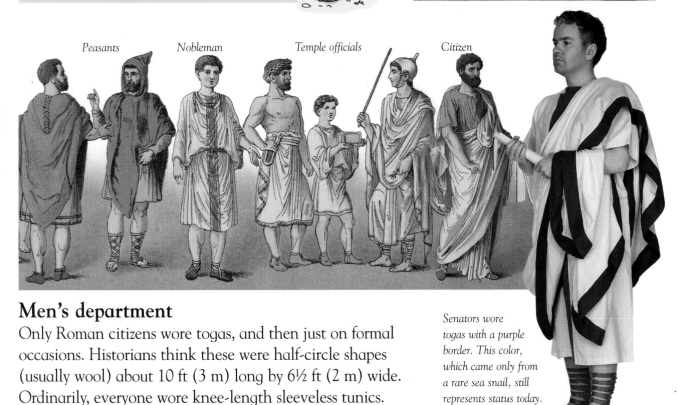

Peasants   Nobleman   Temple officials   Citizen

Men's department

Only Roman citizens wore togas, and then just on formal occasions. Historians think these were half-circle shapes (usually wool) about 10 ft (3 m) long by 6½ ft (2 m) wide. Ordinarily, everyone wore knee-length sleeveless tunics.

Senators wore togas with a purple border. This color, which came only from a rare sea snail, still represents status today.

Mealtime

Like us, the Romans had three meals a day. Breakfast and lunch were small and quick—maybe just bread and fruit. The main meal of the day was a large, leisurely dinner. Eaten in the late afternoon, it was an important social event for family and friends.

phew! *eenw!*

Herbs

Salt

Smelly sauce

Because food spoiled very quickly, people used sauce to disguise its taste. The favorite was *garum*, made from fish (guts, blood, and everything else), salt, and herbs— all mashed in a pot and left to rot.

Fish

Fish guts

Garum factories were far from towns because of the stink.

Ground meat rolled in bread crumbs

Finger food

People ate with their fingers or with spoons—there were knives in the kitchen, but not on the table. Food was served in small pieces and arranged in bowls— diners helped themselves.

Fare and fowl

Romans ate lots of things we enjoy—bread and pastry, fish and shellfish, cheese, poultry and meat, eggs, vegetables, and fruits. But they had some strange favorites, too, such as lark tongue and peacock brains.

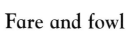

Food facts

● Banquets had so many courses diners would make themselves vomit so they could keep eating!

● Dinner guests took their own napkins—and used them to wrap up leftovers to take home.

● Romans preserved food by pickling, drying, smoking, and salting. This didn't always work, however, so food poisoning was probably common.

Roman kitchens

Food was cooked in pots on flat metal stands or hung from chains over an open fire. Smoke escaped through a small hole in the ceiling or wall. Bread and pastry were cooked in round ovens, and sometimes poor families shared one large, communal oven.

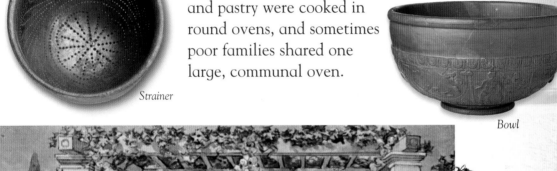

Strainer

Bowl

Knife

Serving slave

Relax and enjoy

Family meals were eaten sitting around a table, but at banquets (attended only by men), diners lounged diagonally on couches. These were placed around three sides of a table, giving access for slaves to bring food and take dishes away.

31

Growing up in Rome

In ancient Rome, children looked (and were expected to behave) just like grown-ups, only smaller. They were considered the property of their fathers, who sometimes kept control of their daughters even after they married.

In this stone sculpture, children are shown as tiny adults. This is just how Roman society saw them.

Fun and games

Roman children played with some of the same toys you do, such as marbles, balls, hoops, model animals, and toy vehicles (chariots, not race cars!).

Stuffed toy

Little girls have always played with dolls. Preserved in the dry soil of Egypt, this simple rag figure is well worn, as if a Roman child loved it very much.

Do you play with marbles that look like these Roman ones?

Home zoo

Family pets were kept mainly for
children. Romans kept dogs and caged
birds, and some people had monkeys,
which they taught to do tricks.

Down for the count

Instead of a calculator, Roman
children used a tool called an abacus
to figure out their math problems.
This one has a surprisingly sleek,
modern look.

*Some Roman letters looked
just like the ones used in
many modern languages.*

Wax tablet

School days

Some children had tutors
at home, but many went
to school for their classes
(below). They scratched
letters on wax tablets (left)
instead of writing on paper.
Boys were given much more
education than girls, who
learned how to run a home.

Stone sculpture of a school

Slave labor

In ancient Rome, people could own other people—adults and children—like they owned animals and furniture, and they could sell or rent them out in the same way. The people who were owned were called slaves.

Slaves for sale

Roman citizens bought slaves in slave markets. The slaves were displayed wearing very few clothes so people could see how strong and healthy they were.

Care and treatment

Many slaves had to wear an identity bracelet. Some were chained, or even branded with a hot iron. Most were treated well, however, since healthy slaves could do more work.

Identity bracelet

Child slaves

Children of slaves often became slaves, too, especially if their parents worked in a large household that they could join. Sometimes, people who weren't slaves were so poor that they sold their own children as slaves.

Hard labor

Slaves did most of the work in every area of Roman life. Some jobs, such as road building (right), mining, and farming, were very hard and tiring.

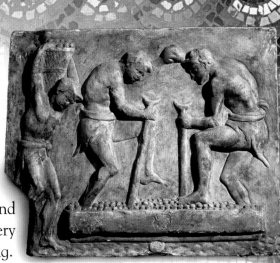

Homework

Domestic work was easier—slaves were often part of the family. They not only cooked, cleaned, and looked after children, but also dressed their owners, did their hair, and carried them through the streets on a handled chair called a litter.

Female slaves dressing their mistress

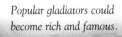

Popular gladiators could become rich and famous.

Freed slaves could not vote, but their children could.

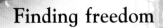

All the slaves in the town of Hesta were freed by this bronze decree in 3 BCE.

Finding freedom

If they raised the money, slaves could buy their freedom. Some did this by taking on the dangerous life of a gladiator or charioteer. Sometimes slaves were freed by their masters.

Country living

In the Roman countryside, there were four basic types of dwelling—the small peasant farm, the grand country house, the big working farm, and the great estate that combined villa and farm.

Olive oil was burned in special lamps to provide light.

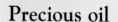

Villa courtyards were large and elegant.

Country retreats

In the Roman Empire, as in many modern countries, wealthy city dwellers kept a country home where they could escape. These villas were much like grand city houses, with gardens and pools.

Precious oil

Olives were a vital crop in ancient Rome. They were a staple food, and they were also pressed to make olive oil, consumed at home and exported widely.

Country facts

● The Romans grew carrots, onions, cucumbers, radishes, figs, cherries, and plums.

● To pick olives, workers shook the tree branches until the fruit fell off—they still do.

● Farmers kept cattle for dairy products, meat, and leather.

Grapes for wine

Grapes were another major crop—some were eaten as fruit, but most were pressed to make wine. The Romans drank wine in large quantities (usually watered down) and shipped it across the empire.

Grapes were picked by hand and put in a large vat. Workers then stamped on them to make juice.

Life on the land

Not all farming was done by rich families who owned lots of land and slaves. Some produce came from peasants who tended very small farms and grew only one or two crops.

This 3rd-century CE mosaic shows farmers plowing in Gaul (Roman France).

Thrill of the hunt

Throughout history, country people have hunted wild animals. Ancient Romans hunted on foot and on horseback—this party used dogs and spears to flush out a wild boar.

Gods and worship

Many religions honor a single, central figure (such as Buddha, God, or Allah), but the Romans had lots of gods. These could even change from one century, or part of the empire, to another. Some emperors were made gods when they died.

Neptune was the god of the sea.

Choose your god

In ancient Rome, there were hundreds of gods, goddesses, demigods, and spirits. Many were adopted from the Greeks or the Etruscans. New gods were added all the time from conquered lands such as Persia and Turkey.

Diana was the goddess of the Moon and of hunting.

Jupiter was the chief Roman god and protector of the empire.

A dedication to Bacchus, the Roman god of wine and drunkenness, is interpreted in a Victorian painting.

Roman worship

Roman towns and cities had many temples, each dedicated to a different god—people would make offerings to the one they needed at the time. Roman religion did not set down specific rules or standards of behavior.

Temples had columns, steps, and a triangular shape called a pediment.

Home help

In each home, offerings were made at a small shrine dedicated to domestic gods and spirits. A man's personal protective spirit was a *genus*, and a woman's was a *juno*.

The spirit of a family's ancestors was a lar.

Early Christian mosaic of the Last Supper.

The coming of Christ

When Jesus first became popular, he was seen as a threat to law and order and killed by the Roman authorities. Christianity was declared illegal, but its popularity spread. By the 4th century CE, encouraged by Emperor Constantine I, it became Rome's official religion.

Trade and transportation

When goods traveled by road, they were loaded onto simple wagons drawn by horses or mules.

One of the reasons the Roman Empire was so prosperous was its incredibly efficient transportation systems. Romans were able to bring in a wide range of goods from the far corners of the empire and send their own products abroad to be sold.

Wine and olive oil were transported in curved pottery jars called amphorae.

Over the waves

Barges and sailing ships were used to transport bulky goods to and from far-away provinces such as Africa and Britain. To protect them from pirates, the Roman navy patrolled the seas.

Roman ports featured elegant architecture and landscaping intended to impress visiting merchants and traders.

Stone model of a ship transporting wine in Germania, modern-day Germany

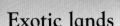

Exotic lands

From the Far East, along the trail known as the Silk Road, came silk from China, perfumes from Arabia (the Middle East), and cotton, precious stones, and dyes such as indigo from India.

Selling spices

Fragrant spices such as saffron, ginger, and nutmeg were brought in from Arabia and India.

Black pepper from India was very popular in ancient Rome. It was even used in sweet dishes.

British metal

In Britain, the Romans mined precious metals such as gold and silver that they made into coins and jewelry. They also dug tin, lead, and iron from the ground.

Egypt was known as Rome's bread basket.

African harvest

Egypt made an important contribution to the empire. It supplied wheat to make bread, and papyrus (made from a wetland plant), which the Romans used as paper.

Northern bounty

Then, as now, most of the world's amber (fossilized tree resin) came from eastern Europe. The Romans used it to make jewelry, which they wore to prevent bad luck.

The empire lives on

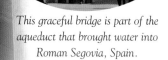

Roman architecture and engineering were so brilliant that many buildings and monuments are still standing today. Some are in ruins, but others look just as beautiful as they did thousands of years ago.

This graceful bridge is part of the aqueduct that brought water into Roman Segovia, Spain.

Baths of Bath

In Britain, the Romans built a city they named *Aquae Sulis* (waters of Sulis, goddess of wisdom). The city is now called Bath, and its baths are still operating today.

African remains

The city of Leptis Magna in Libya is one of the most stunning Roman ruins in the Mediterranean. Its theater attracts thousands of visitors every year.

The Roman Library at Ephesus, Turkey, once held nearly 12,000 scrolls (Romans' equivalent of books). The main reading room faces east to catch the morning sun.

Modern arch

For centuries, the arch of Septimus Severus in Rome's Forum was buried in rubble. Then, in the late 1700s, it was excavated along with the rest of the Forum.

Going strong

The most complete Roman building still in existence is the Pantheon, a domed temple in Rome itself. Built by Hadrian in 125 CE, it became a church in 609 CE, and it still serves as a church today.

Many famous people, including the painter Raphael, are buried in the Pantheon.

Until the 1400s, this was the biggest dome in the world.

CONCRETE ACHIEVEMENTS

One reason Roman structures lasted so long was their solid concrete construction. Although similar materials were used by earlier cultures, the Romans developed their superior concrete— a mixture of lime mortar, sand, stones, and water—to replace stone. Nothing better was invented until the 18th century.

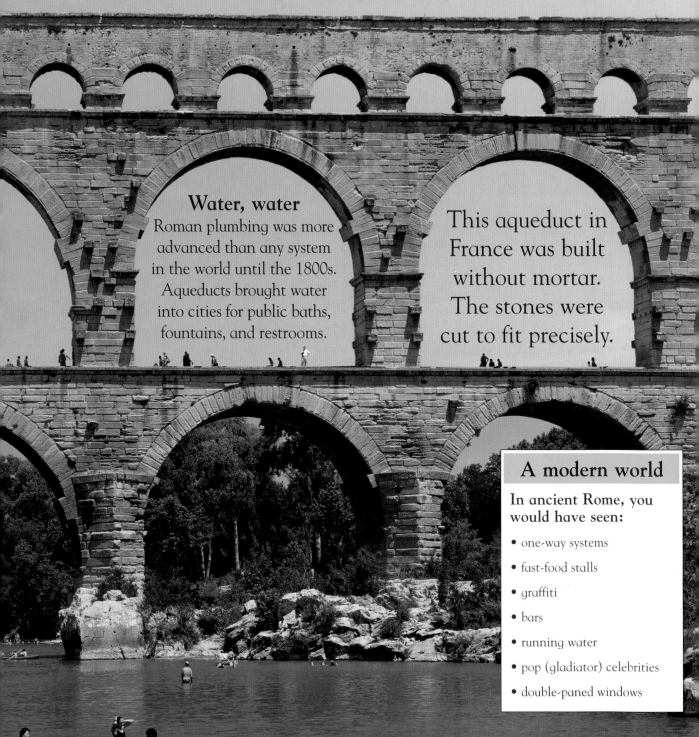

The Romans gave us...

The ancient Romans lived a long, long time ago, so it's easy to think their civilization was basic and primitive. But they were brilliant inventors, engineers, and architects, and they left us a rich legacy of knowledge and technology.

Water, water
Roman plumbing was more advanced than any system in the world until the 1800s. Aqueducts brought water into cities for public baths, fountains, and restrooms.

This aqueduct in France was built without mortar. The stones were cut to fit precisely.

A modern world

In ancient Rome, you would have seen:

- one-way systems
- fast-food stalls
- graffiti
- bars
- running water
- pop (gladiator) celebrities
- double-paned windows

Warm and cozy

In Rome, public baths and the homes of wealthy people were kept warm with complex central-heating systems. These were powered by underground furnaces tended by slaves.

Heat passed under the floor and through spaces in the walls. This warmed the rooms but didn't fill them with smoke.

Month by month

The Romans named the months after their gods and emperors. In many languages, we still use their names today— March, for example, is named for the war god Mars.

The month of August is named after Augustus Caesar.

Word power

We still read and enjoy Roman stories, plays, and poetry. Writers such as Virgil (above center) have provided inspiration and enjoyment for thousands of years.

The Romans replaced dirt tracks with roads that had a strong foundation and several layers.

Roads ahead

The roads we use today are built to a Roman design. Their engineers were the first to make roads domed in the middle, so rainwater could drain away. In countries that were once part of the empire, many roads follow ancient Roman construction.

Race for Rome

Attention legionaries! You have been given orders to race across the Roman Empire to England. Who will be the first to get there?

FINISH
Congratulations, you are the victor!

Look for stones to fill the ballistas. **Move back 4**

Find a path to avoid the Alps. **Move forward 3**

Galley hits rocks off the coast of Spain. **Skip a turn**

Run away from Hannibal's army. **Move forward 4**

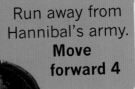

Your armor is stolen! **Move back 5**

Hitch a ride on a chariot. **Move forward 3**

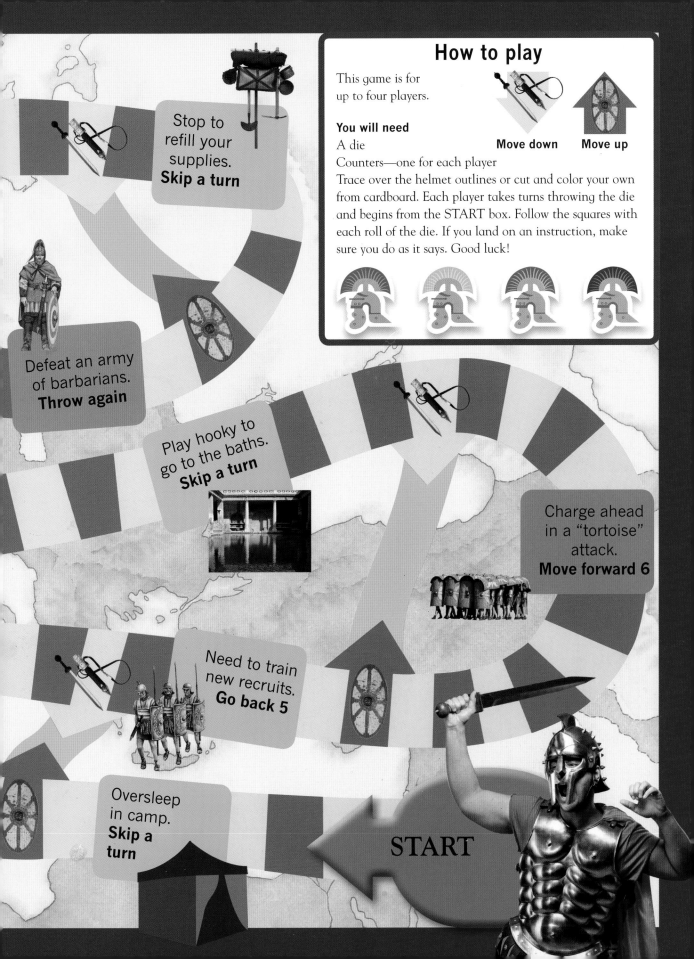

How to play

This game is for up to four players.

Move down   **Move up**

You will need
A die
Counters—one for each player
Trace over the helmet outlines or cut and color your own from cardboard. Each player takes turns throwing the die and begins from the START box. Follow the squares with each roll of the die. If you land on an instruction, make sure you do as it says. Good luck!

Stop to refill your supplies.
Skip a turn

Defeat an army of barbarians.
Throw again

Play hooky to go to the baths.
Skip a turn

Charge ahead in a "tortoise" attack.
Move forward 6

Need to train new recruits.
Go back 5

Oversleep in camp.
Skip a turn

START

True or false?

It's time to test your knowledge of ancient Rome. Spot whether these statements are true or false. Give it a try!

Queen Boudicca was killed by a Roman soldier.
See page 10

Olive oil was burned in special lamps to provide light.
See page 36

The month of August is named after Augustus Caesar.
See page 45

An enormous bridge was built by Hadrian to keep out the Pict tribe.
See page 8

Tigers were common pets in Roman homes.
See page 33

Romans ate peacock brains.
See page 30

Fortune-tellers could "predict" the future by looking at fish guts.
See page 17

To be a citizen of Rome, one had to appear in the official census.
See page 5

Precious metals such as gold and silver were mined in France.
See page 41

The Roman army took six hours to build a complex city for camping.
See page 13

The formation Roman soldiers made to protect themselves was known as a "porcupine."
See page 15

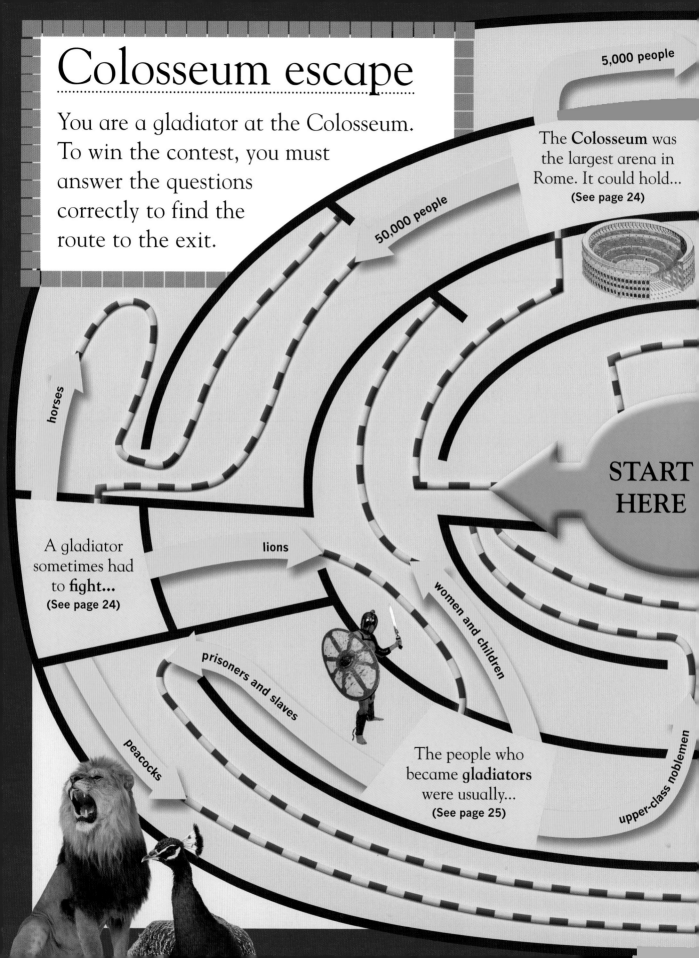

Colosseum escape

You are a gladiator at the Colosseum. To win the contest, you must answer the questions correctly to find the route to the exit.

5,000 people

The **Colosseum** was the largest arena in Rome. It could hold...
(See page 24)

50,000 people

horses

lions

women and children

A gladiator sometimes had to **fight**...
(See page 24)

prisoners and slaves

peacocks

The people who became **gladiators** were usually...
(See page 25)

upper-class noblemen

START HERE

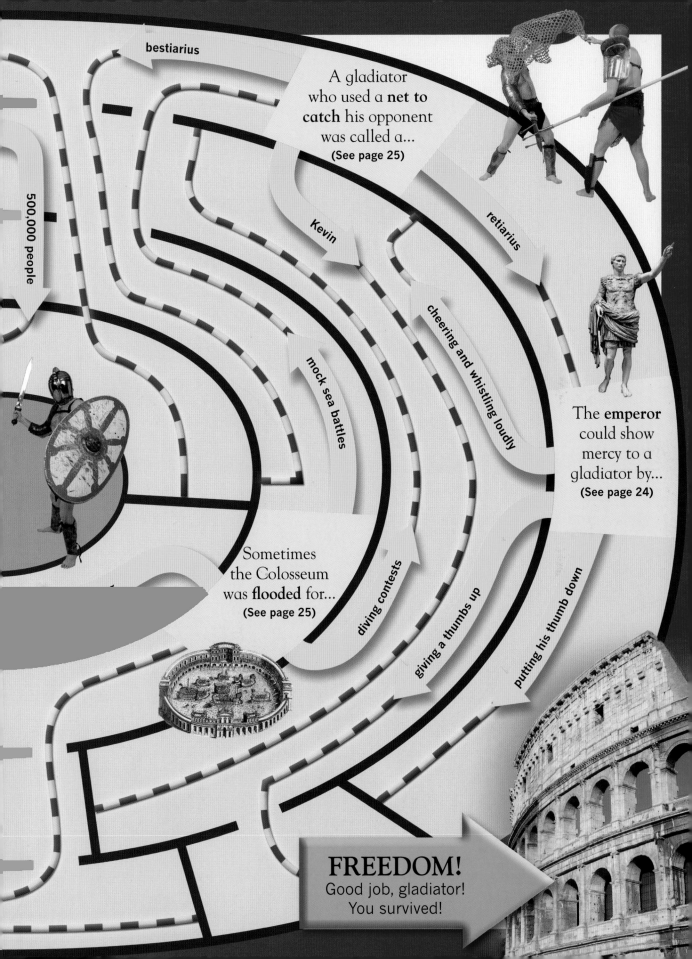

bestiarius

A gladiator who used a **net to catch** his opponent was called a...
(See page 25)

500,000 people

Kevin

retiarius

mock sea battles

cheering and whistling loudly

The **emperor** could show mercy to a gladiator by...
(See page 24)

Sometimes the Colosseum was **flooded** for...
(See page 25)

diving contests

giving a thumbs up

putting his thumb down

FREEDOM!
Good job, gladiator!
You survived!

Facts matchup

How much have you learned about ancient Rome? The answers to these facts can all be found in the pictures.

Black pepper

Theater mask

Wrestling sculpture

Wax tablet

Roman pack

Ballista

Dice

Standard bearer

Romans allowed only upper-body contact in this sport they adopted from the Greeks. See page 22

Set in gold, this beaded jewelry was worn by wealthy women. See page 29

Roman children used it instead of a calculator for math problems. See page 33

Roman soldiers used this to carry their equipment. When full, it could weigh up to 90 lb (40 kg)! See page 12

This mineral was often made into jewelry. It was believed to prevent bad luck. See page 41

This was made from metal strips fastened with leather. Soldiers helped each other to lace it up. See page 13

Many famous men, including the painter Raphael, are buried in this building. See page 43

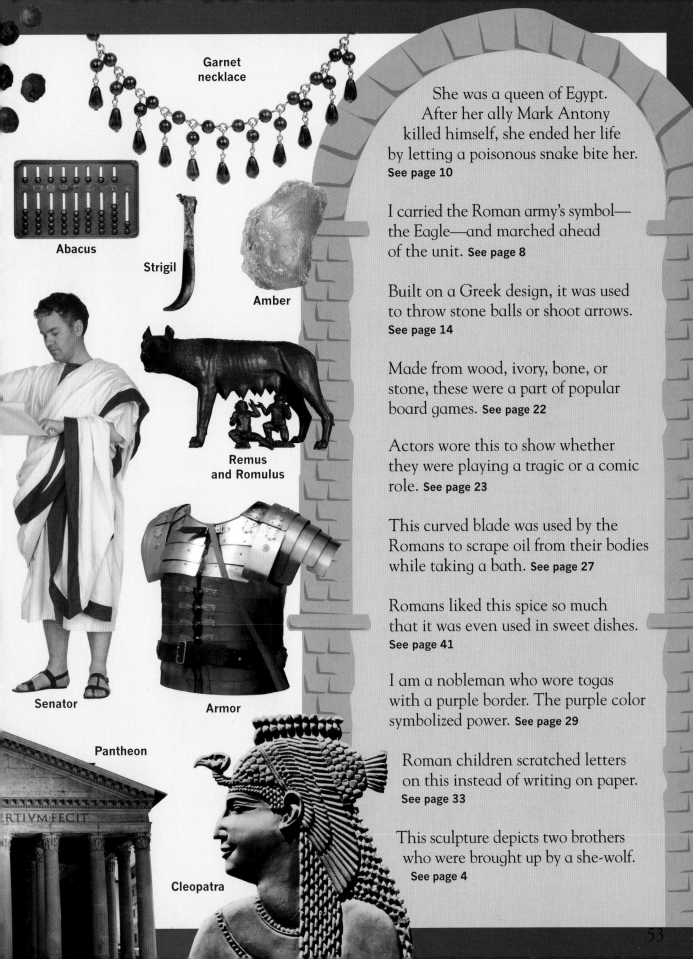

Garnet necklace

Abacus

Strigil

Amber

Remus and Romulus

Senator

Armor

Pantheon

RTIVM FECIT

Cleopatra

She was a queen of Egypt. After her ally Mark Antony killed himself, she ended her life by letting a poisonous snake bite her. See page 10

I carried the Roman army's symbol— the Eagle—and marched ahead of the unit. See page 8

Built on a Greek design, it was used to throw stone balls or shoot arrows. See page 14

Made from wood, ivory, bone, or stone, these were a part of popular board games. See page 22

Actors wore this to show whether they were playing a tragic or a comic role. See page 23

This curved blade was used by the Romans to scrape oil from their bodies while taking a bath. See page 27

Romans liked this spice so much that it was even used in sweet dishes. See page 41

I am a nobleman who wore togas with a purple border. The purple color symbolized power. See page 29

Roman children scratched letters on this instead of writing on paper. See page 33

This sculpture depicts two brothers who were brought up by a she-wolf. See page 4

53

Glossary

Here are some words that are useful to know when you're learning about ancient Rome.

amphitheater an oval arena, usually in the open air, where gladiators fought. The Colosseum is an amphitheater.

aqueduct a special channel (either raised up or buried underground) that carried water into Roman towns and cities.

atrium the central hall of a Roman house; it was open to the sky. Most rooms opened off the atrium.

barbarians a term used to describe unfamiliar people who were thought to be coarse, wild, and uncultured.

catapult a machine used during a siege to hurl stones and darts at, or over, enemy walls.

centuria a company of about 100 men in the Roman army. Each centuria was led by an officer called a centurion.

circus a round or oval stadium where chariot races were held.

citizen a free man, as opposed to a slave. Citizens had many rights and privileges, including the right to vote. (See also slave)

cohort a subdivision of the Roman army. Each cohort contained three manipuli. (See also manipulus)

couch a backless seat, sometimes with ornate ends, on which Romans relaxed at home and reclined to eat formal meals.

emperor the absolute ruler of an empire. "Emperor" was a higher rank than "king." Augustus Caesar became the first Roman emperor in 27 BCE.

forum the main market square, surrounded by public buildings, in a Roman town or city. Public business, as well as trade, was conducted there.

garum a strong-tasting sauce made from rotten fish, salt, and flavorings.

gladiator a trained fighter (usually a slave or a prisoner) who battled other gladiators or wild animals to the death in public contests.

laurel wreath a circle woven from the leaves of a kind of bay plant, to be worn on the head of a leader. A laurel wreath symbolized power.

legion the main division of the Roman army. Each legion contained 10 cohorts. (See also cohort)

legionary a soldier in the Roman army. (See also legion)

manipulus an army unit consisting of two centuriae. (See also centuria)

mosaic a decorated wall or floor made from small pieces of glass, stone, or tile cemented into position. Mosaics can make a picture or a pattern. (See also tesserae)

papyrus an Egyptian water reed whose stem was pressed and dried to make the paperlike sheets Romans wrote on.

peristyle a garden surrounded by columns, and often found behind a grand Roman house.

province a Roman territory that was far from the city. The people who already lived there were called "provincials."

relief a carved or molded image that stands out from its background.

republic a state where power is held by the people or their representatives through voting, rather than by a king or an emperor.

slave a man, woman, or child who is owned by another person as property, usually to do work of some kind.

standard a flag or small statue that is the emblem of an organization, often an army or military unit.

tesserae the small pieces of stone, glass, or tile that are used to make a mosaic. (See also mosaic)

toga the formal garment worn by Roman citizens. It consisted of a length of fabric, usually white, wrapped around the body and draped over one shoulder.

tunic a simple top, tied at the waist and reaching the knees.

villa a luxurious house belonging to a wealthy Roman family.

Index

Acknowledgments

Dorling Kindersley would like to thank:
Andy Cooke for his original illustrations; Penny Smith, Joe Harris, Fleur Star, Nellie Greenwood, and Carrie Love for editorial help; Gemma Fletcher, Mary Sandberg, and Sonia Moore for design assistance.

Picture credits